S0-BTC-056

The Wishing Tree

THE WISHING TREE SERIES

THE WISHING TREE SERIES

The last farmers' market of the season was winding down. Vendors folded their tables to fit in flatbed trucks and wrapped their tents with Velcro straps. What hadn't been sold would be canned for use over the winter.

It had been that way year after year, decade after decade. It had changed, though. What was once a market of necessity—long before there was a grocery chain just up the road—was now a haven for upscale travelers finding weekend respite in the green hills of Vermont. So it was no longer just cucumbers, onions, and tomatoes that graced the booths. It was handmade soaps with aromatic scents that seemed unnatural in their combination but were quite delightful when given a chance. Special combinations like lavender and charcoal or rosemary and eucalyptus to entice the senses. And the unlikely yet interesting partnership of oats and coffee grounds to exfoliate your skin into baby-like softness. Even honey was not exempt from tinkering. It had to be *infused* with cherries and chocolate and cinnamon.

The travelers lapped up the offerings like thirsty kittens paying a king's ransom for local goodies. But it was a mutually beneficial arrangement. Those escaping from the busy, smog-filled cities were buying not only the products but the memories. The fresh air. The peace.

And the locals earned enough to tide them over for the cold season. Sure, Linden Falls still attracted its share of winter playground visitors who enjoyed the slopes that towered over the town at their base. But the market went into hibernation during that time.

Neva had seen more seasons pass in Linden Falls, Vermont, than she cared to remember. If a tree's age could be determined by the rings in its trunk, Neva's could be calculated by wrinkles and liver spots. All the people from her childhood resided in the graveyard on the outskirts of town. None of the living residents could remember a time when Neva Cabot wasn't an intricate part of the town's landscape.

She had attended every wedding, every baptism, every birthday party of every resident. Or so it seemed. She was present in old Polaroid and Brownie camera family photos. And then the digital revolution that negated the need for film put a whole new spin on photography. And now the unimaginable—people taking pictures with their *telephones!* What would they think of next?

Ever since her hair was long and golden and her skin as clear as the water beneath the falls, Neva had owned the bed-and-breakfast on the corner of the town square. It was an old stone building that had been in ruins, save for some intact windows that faced east. When the sun rose, its red hues made it look like the edifice was on fire, mirrored in that pristine glass. In the summer, morning came around four o'clock and, in the winter, almost lunchtime.

But whenever it came, its brilliance shone on the thing the town was most famous for: *the Wishing Tree*.

The lore of the magnificent linden tree that gave the town its name far predated Neva, just as it had far predated her mother. If one had to guess, the tree itself was likely a hundred fifty years old. Its stories and its secrets probably hailed back to when it had grown enough to shelter someone in its shade.

There were many versions of what gave it its reputation. However, most of the townspeople believed the romantic connotation—a long-ago woman's tears watered the roots, shed for a lover who'd gone off to fight the South. And when he returned—remarkably uninjured—she credited the tree with this miracle.

So it had been deemed miraculous. Magical, even. But Neva knew the truth. The tree was neither miraculous nor magical. The tree was a place where the best of humanity revealed itself, and *that*, indeed, was its power.

Neva had left her first wish tied to the tree's branches when she was six years old. She desperately wanted a bicycle, but her family couldn't afford one. The very next day, there appeared at her front door a shiny silver one. Not new—there were dots of rust on its rims—but clean enough. And with a red bow tied to the handlebars. There was no note, and as it was two weeks past Christmas, she thought that perhaps Santa Claus had forgotten it and brought it to her belatedly.

Only later did she learn that Bud Hargraves, the auto mechanic, had seen her place the wish, read it, and polished up the bicycle that his daughter had long ago outgrown.

She came to understand then, as one does when they realize that there are no tooth fairies or leprechauns, that it is hopefulness that leaves the wishes, patience that waits for them, and kindness that grants them. And the people behind those sentiments are the true miracles.

Over the years, she'd seen the wishes increase until sometimes one might think it had snowed in July. The branches filled with scraps of paper wishing for a job, the recovery of an ill spouse, an unrequited love, help with a mortgage payment, and every need that pulls at the human heart.

People visited, and bought their flavored honeys and scented soaps, and left a wish. And others took a wish with the intention of granting it. If not for the exact person, then someone they knew who might need something similar.

Neva knew of a financial advisor in Boston who selected a wish that someone had left hoping to not be alone for Thanksgiving. So he'd discussed it with his wife, and they opened their large home to strangers that holiday and made it a tradition from there on. Neva trusted that that act of generosity had somehow made its way to the stars and then fallen upon that unknown wish-leaver and that whomever she was, she'd been invited to someone's home.

When you put goodness into the world, it manifests itself in ways that you never see.

She'd seen it happen too many times to believe otherwise.

Besides being the oldest woman in Linden Falls and the owner of the Wishing Tree Inn, Neva had another title: Curator of Wishes. It was not an official moniker, and it was something she'd taken on herself for purely practical purposes. When rain clouds or snowflakes darkened the sky, she'd head out to the tree and pluck the wishes from its branches. She'd bring them back to the inn and carefully place each one in a protective plastic sleeve. From there, she put them in binders, cataloged by month and year.

She had decades of them in her cellar. Her treasures. Her bequeathment to Linden Falls. For she knew in her bones that her time was coming to pass and that it would be for someone else to preserve the wishes. It might be months. Or even another year. No one could live forever. Nor did she want to.

But for the time that she had, she would seek to find another to take her place. Perhaps a traveler, entranced by the charm of the town and enticed to stay. Or perhaps a local. She knew them all and had her ideas of who might be an ideal caretaker of this unique history.

Of this she was certain: the legacy of the Wishing Tree of Linden Falls would continue forever. She would make sure of it.

※》》

Read on for a quick preview of the first six books in The Wishing Tree series.

I WISH

AMANDA PROWSE

I WISH

Verity pulled a tissue from the box and blew her nose before reaching for the wineglass and sipping the fruity red that in recent days was more medicine than anything else. It was becoming a habit. Oh, the irony! She had lost count of the number of times she had nagged her husband for coming home at the end of a busy service and reaching for the corkscrew. The sound of a cork leaving the bottle was one that set her teeth on edge. Yet every day for the past week, she had done precisely that. Anything to block out the pain and sharp detail that played in her mind on a loop.

Tripping over the cobbles in the dark and ferreting for her key in her handbag as she arrived at their Bijoux mews house in the heart of London's Chelsea, she grappled with the key in the lock for what seemed like an eternity. Finally, she got the door open and headed straight for the kitchen. This, another small and inevitable change of her newfound circumstances:

she never used to carry keys, always standing back to let him open the door and flick on the lamp, the man of the house, guardian of her safety.

When she had first met Sonny, almost twenty years ago now, his constant attention had driven her crazy. She had been a fully functioning grown-up, keys and all! His arrogant assumption that he should be the one to drive, walk on the curb to shield her from traffic, and check the doors and windows before retiring, as if she were a little less than capable, a little weaker than he, was the source of many a row. The kind of row you had when things were new, emotions ran high, and you were still figuring out how the two of you worked as a couple. His actions left her feeling conflicted: she welcomed them at some level yet simultaneously found them diminishing. How she hated to feel reliant on this slightly older, confident man, and yet she was warmed by it too. It was dangerous ground, showing the kind of vulnerability that could get a girl hurt. In recent years, not only had she grown used to him taking the lead, but she kind of liked it too, seeing it, eventually, not as a lessening of her capabilities but rather something that allowed her to think of other things. A freedom of sorts to live without the burden of worry over such trifles.

Sonny took care of household security, the paying of bills, and any other administrative tasks. And she had come to like living under his muscled wing, where routine and familiarity welcomed her home. And here she was, having reluctantly given up the small freedoms of a life lived alone and yet, in that moment, yearning for his presence and those very interventions she had initially detested.

She shivered, but in this instance the chill was nothing an extra jersey or thick pair of socks could fix. It was the bone-deep chill of rejection. She felt cut loose, adrift, surplus to requirements, and it didn't feel nice at all. She felt hollow. Today, however, after a busy lunchtime shift at the restaurant, wine was what she wanted. She kicked off her shoes to let her feet, swollen from running around the hot stoves, rest on the cool slate floor. Then headed to the kitchen to pour a glass of red. Sitting at the counter now, balancing on the leather barstool, she balled the soggy tissue and threw it in the general direction of the bin, where it landed on the floor next to the cat's bowl. Not that she had seen the cat for a couple of days.

'You too, eh, Wordsworth?' Tears of self-pity stung the back of her throat. She buried her face in her hands. 'I can't go on like this. It's killing me.' Raising her face to the ceiling, she spoke to the ether, reveling in the necessary drama of the moment, knowing she would sink to these depths, give in to the pull of misery, before rising like a phoenix from the flames. She hoped that with some of her verve restored, her heart, although not exactly healed, might be taped together enough to hold.

It was the worst of situations. She and Sonny had started the restaurant together. They had bought, reno-vated, and furnished the house together. They had welcomed their now teenage daughter, Sophie, into the world together. And they had even chosen Wordsworth from the shelter— together. Theirs was a life entwined, knitted with all they had experienced and all they had shared into a blanket that she had thought kept them cosy, safe, and warm. This was not the case for Sonny, apparently. According to the words rushing from his dry, nervous lips as they closed up the restaurant only ten days before, he had been *slowly suffocating, their living "situation" stifling his creativity and sucking the joie de vivre from his soul...*

'What do you mean exactly?' She had stared, expecting a punch line, completely unaware that they had or were in a "situation."

'I mean'—he looked over her head, as if by concentrating on the life beyond the window of their successful eatery, he could picture a new, different life, which gave him the confidence to spit out all that had been seemingly stoppered in his throat for God only knew how long— 'I feel...' He paused and narrowed his eyes, rolling his hands in the way he did when trying to describe something exactly, usually food, the detail and precision of which was important to him, to them both.

'We need to amplify the umami...

'It should be cold but not cold, soft cold, not ice cold...

'We want it the pale colour of apricot cream; this has hues of yellow. Start again...'

Verity had stared at him, waiting to see what came

next, keen to understand how he was feeling and what he needed to say and keener still to get home to a hot shower and a soft mattress, as the day's fatigue snapped at her heels and pulled her limbs until they felt brittle.

'I feel that we are at the end of our path. We need to find new routes and I think we need to navigate them separately.'

'What are you talking about?' She laughed then, a guttural sound that was instinctive because this had to be a joke, albeit a bad one.

Sonny had rubbed his brow and she noticed the small peppering of sweat on his top lip. He was nervous. Gone was the confident swagger of the public character. The booming voice that he could summon at will for interviews and the various celebrities visiting his kitchen, grinning broadly for the selfies and the stove shots that would ratchet up 'likes' when shared on social media. It was this attention, this worship that fueled his confidence and gave him an arrogance that was entirely necessary for him to rise to the top in the culinary world. And the top was where he now resided, with not one but two Michelin stars nestling under his name on the shiny brass plate, which sat on the wall by the entrance to the restaurant. The fact that she had been part of the brigade along with Dax, their manager, since the very beginning, or the small matter that it was her parents' investment that got them off the ground in the first place, was never mentioned. Sonny was the star, the driving force, and the talent. In that moment, however, as he struggled for words and avoided eye contact, he looked and sounded more like the old Sonny, the man she'd loved before he found fame and fortune, and were it not for the topic under discussion, she would have been glad for the reminder of it. She sat down hard on one of the dark wooden cross-backed bistro chairs, as if understanding that if she didn't take a chair, there was a very real chance that, as this conversation unfolded, she might fall.

'You are the mother of my child,' he began.

'Yes I remember, fourteen hours of hard labour and so many stretch marks my thighs now look like crepe paper...' she joked to ease the tension. It was a protection of sorts. When her father had died, some two years ago now, she had held her sister's eye line as the news tumbled from her mouth and tutted, 'Typical! I've just ordered his bloody birthday cake! Well, we either find someone called Charles who is about to celebrate his seventy-fifth or it's going in the bin!' before bursting into tears and falling into her sister's arms.

Sonny didn't laugh but took a seat at a nearby table, close enough that she could hear his words, whispered almost, but out of touching distance. It was only later, in the days ahead, that these small details would be considered—once the shock had subsided, and anger began to edge its way into her thoughts.

'You're also my great friend, my business partner.'

'What is this, Sonny? I can't decide if you're about to throw me a surprise party or are practising my eulogy.'

He took a deep, slow breath and ignored her comment.

'You're my great friend but not my lover.' His words were slow and dramatic, practised.

'Oh, God, is this about sex?' She took a deep breath and rubbed her tired eyes. 'I've told you, it's not that I don't find you attractive, but I'm honestly so exhausted when we get home. It's always late and I run during the day without pausing, and as soon as I step inside the front door, it's like my bones go soft and my eyelids are weighted and the next thing I know the alarm is going off, screeching at me to get out of bed and do the whole thing again! I barely have enough energy to spend time with Sophie, and I know it should be more of a priority but...'

'I'm leaving.' Finally, he looked at her. 'I'm leaving, Verity.'

Silence sliced the air around them.

'What do you mean you're leaving? Leaving where?' She looked at the clock above the concrete counter that allowed customers to see into the open kitchen. Did he mean he was going home? She wanted to leave too; it was nearly a quarter to midnight, and if only he would shut up, they could lock the door, pull the shutter, and both call it a night.

'I'm leaving you. Leaving our marriage.'

His words ricocheted around the walls before coming to lodge in her heart like slivers of glass. Her throat felt tight and her words, when they came, sounded strange to her own ears. Conventional wisdom says there must be some clue missed, some hint of the impending implosion of a marriage that many a spouse simply chooses to ignore— but this, she now understood, was not always the case. She had no clue, no warning, no hint. This alone made the thought of separation something unimaginable, almost funny. She had sometimes wondered if, despite his success, he hankered for the island life he left behind nearly two decades ago. Was he heading back to St. Lucia? The place he still called home?

'But...' What did she want to say? *But I love you! But what will it do to Sophie? But what about the restaurant?'*

'It's been in my head for a while,' he cut in before coughing nervously to clear his throat.

'How long is a while?' She swiped at the tears that fell maddeningly down her cheeks as her gut folded. She wanted to be cool, calm, and in control, like the heroine of her own movie who struts and flicks her hair, but her broken heart made no allowance for that. Instead, she wept and crumpled, wearing her sadness like a veil for all to see. It was ugly uncontrolled crying, but a beautiful dedication to the love she had thought was permanent.

The front door closed loudly, as if someone had kicked it shut. The bang drew Verity from her thoughts, for which she was thankful. Even she was starting to find the maudlin reflection a little depressing.

'Hey, Mum!' Sophie called out as she wandered into the kitchen with Wordsworth in her arms.

'Hello, darling! Hello, fat cat!'

'Well, yes, he is fat. Mrs. Roper's been feeding him.'

'No wonder he's not been coming home. At least it wasn't personal.'

'I think she's a bit batty, Mum. She called me Gillian.' Sophie pulled a face.

'Oh, she's not batty, just getting on a bit, and she does love this pussycat.'

Sophie kissed his sweet head before placing him on the floor and took the barstool opposite her mother.

'Please don't cry.'

'I'm not.' She forced a smile. 'I mean, I have been, but I'm not now. I like to get it all out of my system in one hit. And preferably before I see you so as not to make you unduly worried.'

'I am worried, unduly or not.' Her smart girl stared at her, seemingly gathering herself for what came next. 'Dad called today, said we could go for lunch on Sunday somewhere, just the two of us. I think he wants to talk... but if you'd rather I didn't...'

Verity saw the double blink of anxiety and hated that Sophie was in this position, torn between supporting her and spending time with the father she adored. She took her hand. The fact that he had temporarily and swiftly moved out was hard on them both. The echo of him lingered in the hallways and his scent still on his pillow pulled her from sleep.

'Of course, go see your dad, any time! He loves you so much. And that will never, ever change. He may have fallen out of love with me, but never, ever with you. There are two things I'll say about Sonny: he's a great chef and a great dad.' This she knew to be true. Sophie nodded her acknowledgment and Verity saw her shoulders slump a little with relief, as if reassured a little to hear these words.

'I need to tell you something, Mum.'

Verity sat up straight, alerted by her daughter's tone that this was not necessarily something she wanted to hear.

'What is it?'

'It… it was in the papers today.' Sophie bit her lip and tucked her thick, curly black hair behind her ears in the way she did when she was anxious.

'What was in the papers?'

'About Dad. About Dad and you. And about Dad and Freya Walsh.'

'Oh, God, no!' Verity closed her eyes. She had not wanted her daughter to find out about Freya, at least not yet and certainly not via skewed newspaper gossip.

'What did it say?' she hardly dared ask.

'Something like, "Celebrity chef Sonny Joseph has left his wife for sharp-tongued food critic."'

'All right, Soph, I get it.' Her tone was a little harsher than she had intended, as she rubbed her brow.

'You did ask!'

'I did. I'm sorry.' She took a breath. 'Was there a picture?'

'An old one of you and Dad outside the restaurant. You look really young and really happy.'

'I was. Both,' she squeaked, as a fresh batch of tears

gathered. 'So how did that make you feel reading that? Are you okay?'

'It made me a little mad at you and Dad. You don't have to keep things from me, Mum. I'm seventeen!'

Verity felt the hot tears trickle over her cheeks and smiled at her beautiful girl on the cusp of womanhood and yet to her still a baby. Possibly always to her a baby.

'I wish I could run away, Soph. I don't want to be near the restaurant, the house, the press... I wish we could just pack a bag and go.'

'So why don't we?'

Verity laughed out loud. 'Because...'

'Because what? I think it might be good for us to have a change of scenery, just for the summer. I've got nearly three months before school starts again, and you can nap and walk and do all the things you moan you never have time for.'

'You'd miss Dad if we weren't in Chelsea.'

'Mum, I never see him and we live in the same house! Or used to. He's always working or I'm out with my friends. Besides, it's only for the summer!'

'Where would we go?' Verity felt a spark of, if not joy, then certainly relief at the prospect of leaving these familiar streets where the whisper of her husband's infidelity lingered like a shadow on lamplit corners and hung in the morning mist.

'I know!'

Sophie ran into the sitting room and came back with the globe that lived on the drink table.

'I'll give it a good spin and you close your eyes and put your fingers on it. Where they land is where we shall head!'

'God, I'm not sure. We might get Siberia or the middle of a shark-infested ocean!' Her daughter looked a little crestfallen, and the red wine was starting to make her feel a little giddy. 'Okay, Soph! Spin it! Let's do this!'

Verity rubbed her hands in anticipation as her daughter spun their whole wide world. With her eyes closed, she reached out her fingers and tapped down hard. The globe stopped spinning and the two peered at the small space that was in the US.

'America!' Sophie laughed. 'I've always wanted to go to New York!'

'Yes, but this isn't New York, it's'—she narrowed her eyes and lifted the globe to better see the words, written in italics—'Vermont.'

'Vermont? Where's that?'

'I'm not sure, but it's where we are heading!'

'Not really though, Mum! We're only joking right?' Sophie stared at her. 'Surely we're not going to pack up our lives and go and stay somewhere we chose at random from a globe spin, because that would be totally nuts, right?'

Verity felt her face break into a smile, 'It would, darling. It would be totally nuts.'

》》》

Thank you for reading an introduction to *I WISH*, Book 1 of The Wishing Tree series, available here. Keep reading for a glimpse into each of the books in the series. You won't want to miss a book in this wonderful new collection from a group of best-selling authors, who are all founding authors of My Book Friends.

WISH YOU WERE HERE

KAY BRATT

WISH YOU WERE HERE

Neva woke feeling stiff and sore. Getting the house ready for visitors had led to a restless night. For some reason, the little fairy door and its yet unknown bene-factor wouldn't leave her mind. She felt sure the wish for a mom to find a job had probably come from the same person who'd left the little door.

She fixed a cup of coffee and a piece of toast, then settled down at the tiny table in her kitchen. It was her private spot—no guests allowed—and usually where she did her best thinking while she waited on cinnamon rolls to cook or bacon to sizzle.

Myster jumped up on the opposite chair and stared at her over the rim of the table. He knew better than to climb up any farther.

"You don't like toast," she said to him.

His stare was unflinching.

Today, on her last morning with an empty house, she nibbled slowly. And she pondered.

That was the word her grandmother had always used, and the older Neva got, the more the antiquated words found their way into her thoughts and speech.

It was like this, she told herself (not aloud, she wasn't that feeble-minded yet and even if she was, the cats didn't like her talking to herself because it made them nervous) that more times than not in her life, things happened in just the order that they should. A wise man once said there was no such thing as coincidence, and if that was true, she needed to get back down to the tree.

There wasn't any sense in killing herself playing house manager, housekeeper, and everything else that she was juggling when maybe synchronicity was in play and a temporary housekeeper was eager and looking, being advertised by a slip of paper blowing in the wind.

Neva knew her talents could be used much better elsewhere. Let someone else make the beds and carry the laundry. Mop the endless floors. And lordy, ironing those sheets had about done her in.

Her aching body perked up in agreement with the way her thoughts were going, sending her signals of urgency to hurry and figure it out.

Of course, there was always the fact that she liked to help as many wishes come true as were possible within her limited reach.

This one—easy cakes.

And possibly more for her sake than that of anyone

else, but no one but her and the old tree needed to know that.

That being decided, she finished her coffee and toast, then rose and put her dishes in the sink. Just this once she'd leave them for washing up later.

"I'll be back soon," she said to Myster, then went out the back door and headed for the town square.

On the way, she tried to decide what she would offer as pay and how she'd talk someone into taking a temporary position. And what if the mom had already found a job? That would be deflating because now Neva already had her hopes set for having help.

She arrived at the square quickly, mostly by keeping her head down and walking with a determined gait that warded off anyone who'd seen her and considered engaging in chitchat. Usually Neva was all about friendliness, but there was no time for any of that today.

A woman on a mission.

Now a woman instantly disappointed. She could see as she approached the tree that there weren't any new wishes, and more importantly, the hope that the owner of the fairy door would be there was dashed.

"Now what?" she asked the tree, her hands on her hips.

A sudden wind stirred up and tousled her scarf, then grabbed it and unwrapped it from around her neck, and before Neva could grab it, it had blown off her completely and was tumbling away.

I do not have time for this, she mentally scolded the tree as she took off after the scarf.

It picked up speed and floated through the air, a bright blue and turquoise waving banner teasing her to chase. Then it settled to the ground, right at the feet of Calvin, their town newspaper reporter.

He bent and picked it up, then stood and smiled at her as she crossed the street toward him, a bit out of breath.

"Thank you, Calvin."

When she reached him, he handed her the scarf.

"My pleasure, Ms. Cabot. What are you up to this fine day, other than chasing scarves around?"

Neva loved that he knew his manners when addressing his elders. She tucked the scarf back around her neck.

"I was hoping to run into someone at the tree."

"Oh? Anyone special?"

She really did feel affection for Calvin, but with his always probing questions and tendency to investigate everything, sometimes she wished he'd just say hello and move on. But he meant no harm and she was never one to tell fibs.

"Just whomever put the fairy door there," she answered, keeping to herself that she had an inkling it was the same person who'd hung the wish.

"Oh, I can help you on that one. It was a little girl named Breeze. I talked to her yesterday."

Now Neva was glad her scarf had decided to seek its freedom and land where it had.

"Who does she belong to?" she asked, trying to keep the excitement out of her voice. Calvin was always looking for a story.

"I'm not sure but she said she lives in the Johnsons' old place. They decided to rent it out until they can figure out what to do with it. I'm not too sure how long that will go for, as the historical society committee is already vying to make it a rule that none of the houses can be used as rentals."

Neva nodded, eager to get going.

"I can understand that, but surely she knows that an empty house will do nothing but rot. It has been looking rather sad lately, don't you think? A home has to have life within its walls, or it will simply want to stop existing. As long as the tenants take good care of the home, I don't see the problem."

He shrugged and, like a good reporter, didn't let his preference show through. Unbiased, he liked to claim.

"Well, anyway, I need to run. Thank you, Calvin. For grabbing my scarf and for the information. Have a wonderful day."

"Same to you, Ms. Cabot." And with that he went on his way, and Neva turned around, heading for the Johnson house, which was only a minute or two away.

In her haste, she nearly ran into Faith and Penny coming out of the Crooked Porch. They were working their lids down onto the disposable cups they carried and weren't looking either.

"Oh, excuse us, Neva," Faith said. "We weren't paying attention."

"Sorry, we were deep in conversation about planning new activities for the center," Penny said. "Have you been recently?"

They both worked at the senior care center where Neva volunteered.

"No, not lately," she said. "But I may see you soon. Right now, I've a lot going on and need to run."

They waved her on and went back to their conversation, leaving Neva to continue around the corner and up the street a piece.

At the house, she paused, standing in front of the old picket fence, and wondered if she could be lucky enough to get a warm welcome and, even better, to find a woman who still needed a job and didn't mind dirtying her hands with housework to earn her way.

Or maybe she hesitated because she wasn't a fan of rejection.

Either way, she paused for so long that before she could make the first move and open the gate, a small, freckled face peeked out the window.

Neva waved.

The girl waved back.

That was a good enough start, so she opened the gate and approached the door, a polite smile pasted to her face.

The girl opened the door, though obviously being a smart little thing, she kept the storm door closed between them, and hopefully locked. Linden Falls was a safe town, but one could never be too careful, and she was a proponent of teaching children to be aware but not suspicious.

"Is your mom home?" Neva asked through the glass.

The girl nodded and quickly disappeared from view.

Another girl took her place.

Definitely too young to be a mother, and more likely a big sister, judging by the same freckles that scattered across her nose. But this girl was a teenager, and one eager for a break in the monotony obviously, because she immediately unlocked the door and opened it.

"Hi. Can I help you?" she asked.

"Yes. Definitely," said Neva. "I'd like to talk to your mom if she is available."

"She's asleep."

"Oh." Neva wasn't sure what to say. It was well past time in the morning that people usually slept. Maybe the mother was sick?

"Is your father home?"

"He doesn't live with us right now."

Hmm. A single mom. Not unusual, though. Not in this day and time when there were so many broken families.

She spotted some stacked boxes behind the girl. Other than that, a faded old couch that had several holes and a shabby armchair to match. She supposed renting the house out to strangers was one thing, but old man Johnson's children must not have wanted them using the furnishings, too, because she remembered much nicer pieces the last time she'd been in the house.

"I see you've just moved in," she said.

The girl turned and looked, then sighed as she nodded.

"Yeah. I mean, yes, ma'am. Sort of."

The younger sister peeked around. "Carly is mad. She hates it here."

"Shut up, Breezy." Carly, as her sister had outed her, blushed, the pink spreading across her freckles even as she shook her head in denial.

"You just said so," the younger girl said.

Neva broke in, hoping to avoid a full-on squabble. She hadn't broken one of those up since the Johnson brothers had last gone to fisticuffs in her Sunday school class.

"It's okay if you don't like it. No one likes moving at your age. Leaving your friends and probably your school," Neva said, trying to be gentle. "I'm sure it was a hard thing to do."

"I don't hate it here. It's not the place. It's just…well, everything." Carly swept her glance around the sparse living room, and when she looked back, there was a sheen of tears in her eyes that she furiously tried to blink away.

Neva's heart lurched. She could feel it in that way that sometimes she just knew things. She was looking at a girl who was at the end of her rope, and not only that but her gut told her this was a family in trouble. She really didn't have the time to spare, but didn't things usually end up coming together in the end?

"Why don't I come in and help you for a bit?" Neva suggested. "I swear I'm just a harmless old lady. I mean, both of you could clobber me from behind and tie me up if you really needed to."

That made them both smile and Carly stepped aside, allowing Neva to come inside. She stepped in gingerly and looked around a bit more. The place was much more run-down than she remembered it.

"So, your mother is sleeping. Does that mean she's been working? Maybe somewhere second shift?" She couldn't think of anywhere in town that offered other shifts, and she hoped she was wrong.

She supposed their father was at work.

"No," Carly said. "She's just taking a break. From looking."

"For a job," Breeze added.

Again, Neva was glad she'd followed her gut.

"How long have you been here?" she asked.

"A few weeks," Carly said.

Weeks? Neva was a bit surprised, considering the limited progress they'd made.

"Mom said we can't stay," Breeze said.

Carly put her arm around her sister and cupped her hand over her mouth, then hissed at her to be quiet.

They were both quite delightful, Neva thought to herself. Even in the teenager's irritation with her sister, you could still see they were close.

"What's going on here?"

Neva whipped around to see a young woman standing in the hall that led to the bedrooms. Disheveled but dressed in a colorful fringed wrap over worn jeans and several layers of necklaces made with colorful stones, she leaned on the doorframe to the living room and crossed her arms. The big, hooped earrings caught the sun when she moved, and her alabaster skin was striking against her jet-black hair.

She looked very...*boho*, Neva supposed the word was.

"They're in online learning, if you're here to see why they aren't in school."

Breeze started to say something, but Carly's hand was quicker, and it popped right over whatever words were ready to slide out.

"Oh, no, I'm not from the school. I'm just a neighbor, checking in."

"Which house?" she asked.

Neva looked out toward the street. "Well, it's a couple of streets over. To be honest, I heard your family had moved into this house, and I thought I'd come welcome you to Linden Falls."

She remembered she should've been carrying a cake or a pie. In her excitement she'd completely forgotten her usual hospitable manners.

"I wanted to make you something, but first thought I'd see if you'd rather have a casserole or a pie?"

"Pie," Breeze said.

"Casserole," Carly corrected her, already looking hungry.

"No worries, we're fine," their mother said. "But thank you for the thought."

She was a tough one.

"I'm sorry. Let me introduce myself. I'm Neva Cabot, the innkeeper." She held her hand out, ready to shake properly.

Her words stopped the young woman short.

"The innkeeper?"

Neva pulled her hand back in, seeing how it wasn't going to be accepted. "Yes. And you are?"

"Is there more than one inn here in Linden Falls?" she asked.

"No, just the one. We've been here for at least a hundred years. I took it over after both of my parents passed."

Carly shot her mom an embarrassed look.

"Mom, she asked your name," she whispered.

"Janie. Janie Stallard."

It was said as a challenge, but Neva wasn't sure why. What she did know was that the name fit her. Stallard meant valiant, or resolute, and this young woman appeared to be the epitome of resolute.

Determined. Unwavering.

Or at least that's what Neva was getting from her serious expression and searching eyes.

But what was she searching for?

Neva had a feeling she'd never tell. And she wasn't one to pry. It would all come out in its own time. She'd learned that over the span of her lifetime.

It always did.

She smiled. "Well, Janie Stallard, welcome to town. I hope you'll all just love it here. I can tell you all kinds of things the local kids like to do and point out the best places to hike to avoid tourists. I mean, if you'd like me to."

Janie shook her head. "No need. I don't think we'll be staying."

"Oh? Leaving so soon?" Neva had said she wouldn't pry, but the question escaped her lips before she could stop it.

"I don't want to," Breeze said, her voice wistful. "I like this town. It has a magical tree."

"It's not magic," Carly said. "There's no such thing as magic. It's a tourist attraction. Stop acting like an eight-year-old."

"I *am* an eight-year-old."

"Girls, please. I can't take your bickering today." Janie sighed, uncrossed her arms, and went to sit in the armchair. She pulled her legs up and gathered her arms around them, looking like a sullen teenager herself, though she had to be at least in her mid-thirties.

"So, you're not staying?" Neva asked.

"I'm sure when the town grapevine gets going this morning, you'll already know. I had hoped to find a job by now and I haven't. So, I can't pay next month's rent. It took all we had to pay the rental deposit and the first month, and I called the landlord last night and told him we'd just go."

"Oh, I'm so sorry," Neva said. She looked around at

the couch. "Mind if I sit for a moment? I'm feeling a little weak."

She went to the couch and sat down. She wasn't really feeling weak.

Well, maybe just a little.

It was called stalling.

The thought of this small family being put out into the street gave her a feeling of dread. Maybe even a bit more than she should have, considering she didn't even know them.

"I'm glad," Carly said. "We can't even get hot water for more than one of us to take a shower each day. And there are mice."

"And spiders," Breeze said, cringing. "I found one in my bed last night."

"She screamed loud enough to wake the neighbor, and he ran over here in his flowered jockey shorts, with a butcher knife in his hand," Carly said, grinning.

Breeze laughed.

"It wasn't funny, girls. They already don't want us here."

Neva could just imagine Old Man Kurz hurrying over in his underpants, thinking he'd save the day.

"Well, at least he wanted to help," she offered.

"He called us ridiculous city people when we told him it was a spider," Breeze said. "And we aren't from the city. I just don't like spiders."

Neva held her tongue though everything in her wanted to ask where they did come from. Janie looked ready to cry, and Neva still wanted to try to get her to take the job.

"I don't want to pry"—(well, actually she did, but she wouldn't)— "but if you really do want to stay, I have a position open at the inn. At least temporarily, until my housekeeper comes back."

Janie tilted her head back and looked at the ceiling. "So, this is what fate wants to do to me? Should I laugh at the irony or cry at the thought?"

Neva wasn't sure if the question was for her or the man upstairs, but she didn't know how to answer it and was confused as to how irony could play into any of it.

"Mom, please take it," Breeze said. "Maybe we can stay. You said just last night that we didn't have—"

Janie's head snapped forward. "Hush. Don't tell our business."

She turned her attention to Neva. "What does it pay?"

"Hmm... I hadn't thought that through yet. Maybe you could come and tour the place, go over the duties, and we could talk about it? I have guests coming tomorrow, but I'd be honored to cook a small dinner for the four of us. You know, as a proper welcome to town."

Janie hesitated and Neva could tell she was really struggling with something.

"Mom, we can at least go have a home-cooked dinner?" Carly said, then turned to Neva. "The stove doesn't work here either."

Neva wasn't happy with the situation. How could someone expect rent to be paid for a house that couldn't even offer enough hot water or a working stove for a family?

Ridiculous.

"Fine. I want to see what the place looks like inside anyway. We'll come for dinner, but I'll tell you right now, I don't think I can work there."

Both the girls looked happy enough that Neva put the curiosity out of her mind about why in the world their mother seemed to be carrying some sort of reluctance about the inn.

She stood and clapped her hands together.

"Great. Now, what would you like tonight? Pot roast or spaghetti?"

The girls answered in unison, and thankfully, they agreed.

With a six o'clock dinnertime set, Neva bid them goodbye and hurried out the door. She had work to do and two cats that she needed to persuade to be on their best behavior. Hopefully she could also tempt Janie into taking the job so that when her guests came the next day, everything could be perfectly aligned.

Once again, an air of excitement raced through her blood. She knew the feeling well, though it had been a while since she'd felt it.

For now, her energy was satisfied that she was following the path the universe had laid out for her.

Hopefully, she could stay on it.

＊＊＊＊

Thank you for reading an introduction to *WISH YOU WERE HERE*, Book 2 of The Wishing Tree series, available here. Keep reading for a glimpse into each of the books in the series. You won't want to miss a book in this wonderful new collection from a group of best-selling authors, who are all founding authors of My Book Friends.

WISH AGAIN

TAMMY L. GRACE

WISH AGAIN

The glint of the streetlights reflected off the shiny leaves of the tree—the magnificent linden that graced the square and that Margot had always considered hers, even though it belonged to the entire town of Linden Falls. Sleep eluded her, which was nothing new. She had battled insomnia for the last twenty-odd years. Ever since her hormone levels began to go wonky in her fifties, Margot hadn't had a decent night's sleep.

In the wee hours of this morning, her daughter, Paige, weighed on her mind. She would be coming home to live with Margot this week. The last few days had been filled with excitement in preparation for Paige's arrival. Eager to have her back in the nest, where Margot could help her and boost her spirits, she was counting the minutes, but at the same time, worry niggled at the back of her mind. They hadn't lived under the same roof since Paige graduated college and moved to Albany. Friends who had opened their homes to their adult children lamented the woes and stress it brought. The last thing either of them needed was more stress.

The old clapboard house was plenty big enough, so they'd each have their own space, and Paige loved the bookstore as much as Margot, having grown up in it and finding her own career as an illustrator because of it. Books and stories had brought them many hours of escape and peace, and Margot hoped being surrounded by books and happy memories would comfort her precious daughter. Grief had swallowed her sweet girl, and Margot knew, more than anyone, there was no expiration date as to when the suffocating fog would lift.

She turned to admire the handcrafted sign over the cheerful red door of the entrance to the bookstore. Tom had made it for her all those years ago when he suggested they turn one side of the downstairs into a book shop. Once the children were in school, she'd felt lost, so she buried herself in books. One night she'd mentioned how much fun it would be to own a book-store, and the next thing she knew, Tom had commissioned a contractor and had plans drawn up to make her dream a reality. Ever since, she'd run Town Square Books out of the large house, built in the 1840s, that she and Tom had fallen in love with and bought after they were married.

Her eldest, Jed, ran Duncan's Hardware. Being divorced, he spent far too many hours at the store but always found time to wander over and have dinner with her a few times a week. While she feared it might be out of obligation, she didn't care. She treasured the time she had with her children. It would be good for Paige to reconnect with her big brother, and her presence might tear him away from work more often.

From the swing she had sat in for the last fifty years, on the porch that she cherished, Margot looked out on the sleeping town. She bent and ruffled the top of Gladys's head, running her fingers over the velvety-soft ears of her sweet golden retriever sleeping atop her feet. Her thick fur and body heat kept Margot's bare feet warm.

Save for the soft glow from the streetlights and a light in the window of Neva's bed-and-breakfast, it was dark and quiet along Main Street. Living alone, as she had these last years without Tom, had brought hardships, but she never felt lonely. Linden Falls was home, where she found comfort in knowing every crack in the sidewalk and the ability to identify the buildings that lined the town square and street by their faint outlines against the dark summer sky. It was a place where everyone knew each other and looked out for one another. A true community, where those who craved anonymity would be frustrated, but those looking for a village filled with caring people, more like an extended family, would thrive.

She would hike to the falls, where memories of her youth would accompany her. The best times of her life were embedded in the fabric of the village she called home. The many hours she and Tom had spent sitting in a booth at the old soda fountain and then taking Jed and Paige there for after-school treats filled her heart with joy. The soda fountain was now modernized, incorporating a trendy coffee bar, but still had the best maple creemees in Vermont.

During summer, the constant flow of visitors from the cities, looking for a slice of Americana, kept her and the other shopkeepers busy and infused with cash. Her close group of friends, formed when they met at a grief workshop and discovered they also shared a love of wine, even calling themselves the Winey Widows, checked in on each other and organized trips and outings. The stunning leaves of fall never disappointed and brought busloads of leaf peepers to her quaint village. They filled the town coffers as they lodged, ate, and slept in Linden Falls. Snow fell early and heavily, and although less enthusiastic about winter than when she had been younger, Margot always looked forward to the first snow—the smell, the quiet, and the beauty always amazed her. There was no better time to curl up with a wonderful story and a cup of tea than a snowy Vermont winter day. Unlike her friend Jean and other snowbirds who retreated to sunny Florida for the winters, she couldn't imagine ever leaving this place.

Summer was just beginning, bringing perfect weather and stunning flowers and the promise of a steady stream of visitors who often wandered into the bookstore. The shop provided the best of both worlds —a close connection and gathering spot for the community and a place to interact with visitors passing through, where brief encounters often led to lifelong customers who would call in orders to have them shipped across the country. Jed had finally convinced her to implement an online store to make it easier for customers outside of Linden Falls to place orders. It was more lucrative, but Margot missed chatting with customers when they phoned in their orders.

Summers were busy at the bookstore, and after Labor Day there was a short reprieve before the crazy time from mid-September until late October, when thousands of people traveled through the village in search of fall foliage and, as luck would have it, books. Having Paige here to share the workload would be a welcome respite.

The same breeze that fluttered her hair and jogged her back into the present ruffled the leaves of the Wishing Tree. The sturdy linden tree had always held a special place in her heart. Whether budding in spring, a full canopy of shade in summer, decked out in brilliant leaves for fall, or blanketed in snow during winter, like a lifelong friend, the steady tree was always there. She had grown up believing in the magic of the tree to grant wishes, and as she'd moved into adulthood, married Tom, helped him run the hardware store, and raised their two children, she had witnessed many wishes come true. Despite her beloved tree not seeing fit to honor her wish that Tom be spared, she had never given up hope in its ability to bring about good in the world.

Paige was far more skeptical and, after Tom passed,

had lost all faith in the allure of the Wishing Tree. She couldn't understand how Margot still believed in the folklore that surrounded the tree and its reputation for connecting couples or its power to fulfill the dreams and wishes locals and visitors alike tied to its branches. Paige's practical nature didn't allow much room for the idea of a tree having some type of magical powers.

Margot reached for her book from the side table and pulled out a paper card with a sparkly orange ribbon attached to it. She had been pondering what to write all week. She flipped her mini book light on and, in the same lovely script that lettered signs in the store, wrote her wish for Paige.

She didn't need a watch to know it was nearing five o'clock. The soft glow on the eastern horizon signaled dawn would soon arrive. Jed would be coming by with his sweet golden, Bentley, like he did each morning, to share a cup of coffee before he opened the hardware store. She and Gladys went back inside, where she found her flip-flops and the two of them walked across the square. Margot stood on her tiptoes, stretched and reached for a branch, looping and tying the ribbon onto it. She let it go and the paper bobbed up and down before finding its place to dangle in the tree, along with hundreds of others.

Gladys, so named because she had a nosy tendency and was always snooping around the town square, followed Margot back to the house. Gladys buried her snout in one of the half barrels Margot had filled with flowers that decorated the entrance to the store. As

Margot glanced at the porch, the memory of Paige sitting with her on the porch the night Tom passed was so vivid she swore she could see them, her arm wrapped around her grown daughter, who seemed childlike, as they sat together on the swing. She blinked, startled at the lifelike image. Her eyes were playing tricks on her.

Paige had taken out her anger and frustration on the Wishing Tree, vowing to never trust it again. Her dad had loved her and spoiled her, as men tend to indulge their daughters, and his loss had devastated Paige. Margot and Paige had tied countless wishes to the tree during Tom's illness, hoping for a miracle. The night her father died, Paige had cried and wailed, asking her mother how she could keep believing. Margot had stroked her hair and given her daughter the same answer each time she asked.

As the lavender light of a new day blossomed in the sky, Margot whispered her answer. "Wish again, sweetheart. Wish again."

※》》

Thank you for reading an introduction to *WISH AGAIN*, Book 3 of The Wishing Tree series, available here. Keep reading for a glimpse into each of the books in the series. You won't want to miss a book in this wonderful new collection from a group of best-selling authors, who are all founding authors of My Book Friends.

WORKOUT WISHES & VALENTINE KISSES

BARBARA HINSKE

WORKOUT WISHES AND VALENTINE KISSES

Pam Olson yanked on the handle of the rolling overhead door, sending it to the concrete threshold with a clank. She maneuvered the locking pin into place and secured it with the industrial combination lock she'd bought in the office of the self-storage facility.

It was done. She'd loaded the last remnants of her marriage to Lance Foster into storage. The final decree had been issued, and they'd sold their home. Most of their furnishings had reflected his taste, not hers. She'd taken the few items she wanted. It was now time to move forward into her newly single life.

She was sure of just one thing. Health and fitness were her passion, so she'd continue her career as a personal trainer. But she'd do so somewhere other than Boston. She would decide where to relocate later. Right now all she wanted to do was take a break, rest, and recuperate.

Pam split her dark chestnut ponytail into two plaits and splayed them, tightening the elastic band against her skull. She punched in her mother's phone number on her cell as she walked to her car.

"Pam," Irene said. "Are you on your way?"

"I'm leaving my storage unit now. I'll get gas and grab a coffee before I hit the road."

"Why don't you pick up a sandwich too? I'll bet you haven't had a bite to eat today."

Pam smiled. Her mom had been clucking and fussing over her since Pam broke the news of her impending divorce. "I had a protein shake for breakfast, and I've got energy bars in the car. I'll be fine."

"I've got a pot of chicken noodle soup simmering on the stove, and I'll make a salad with greens from the farmers' market. We can eat as soon as you get here if you like."

"That sounds fabulous, Mom." Irene's chicken noodle soup was one of her childhood favorites. "You spoil me."

"Somebody has to." Irene's voice was full of concern. "I'm glad you're coming to stay with me for a bit, honey. You need time to clear your mind and regroup."

"I'm anxious to get home, Mom. I appreciate your willingness to let me stay with you. I won't be there long—I promise. I'll get my act together and be on my way soon."

"Stay as long as you want. I didn't see you nearly as much as I would have liked to while you were married to that..." Irene paused, considering her words. "Over these past few years."

Pam blinked rapidly. She'd allowed Lance's dislike of Irene to drive a wedge between her and her mother. "I'm...I'm so sorry about that, Mom." Her voice cracked.

"No regrets—about anything!" Irene commanded. "I'll see you when you get here."

Pam walked to her car and clicked the fob to unlock it. "I should be there in three hours, give or take."

"Drive safely."

Pam disconnected the call and stowed her phone in her pocket. She filled her gas tank and bought herself an extra-large coffee at the mini market attached to the gas pumps. Then, on impulse, she snatched up a sleeve of powdered-sugar donuts displayed on a rack at the register.

Back in her car, she took a sip of her steaming coffee and pulled back the wrapper from the donuts. Taking care to contain the inevitable powdered-sugar mess, she popped a donut—whole—into her mouth.

Pam tapped at the screen of her phone to start the playlist of Spice Girls, NSYNC, and Back Street Boys songs she'd created for her drive. If she were returning to her high school stomping grounds, she'd make the trip with a soundtrack from that era. She gobbled another donut, washed it down with coffee, and began to sing along.

Traffic was light on this Thursday afternoon in early fall, and highway signs announcing exits for

Linden Falls appeared at the side of the road while the sun was still high in the sky. Pam checked the clock on her dashboard. She was making excellent time.

The highway exit for her mother's house was a mile ahead. She moved into the right-hand lane but drove past without attempting to pull off. The Linden Falls Town Square was just off the next exit, with her late grandmother's home only a few minutes past the square. It had been years since she'd seen the old house, which had been the setting of so many happy times during her idyllic childhood.

She pulled off the highway and made the short drive to the square. Her heart beat faster as she passed the quaint clapboard homes and brick buildings along her route. The Crooked Porch Café, Town Square Books, and Doc's Fountain—all such prominent parts of her teen years—were still there, open for business. The trees lining the square had donned their fall foliage and would do justice to any chamber of commerce brochure. Linden Falls was the quintessential New England Town.

The linden tree in the center of the square rose taller than the others and was sporting leaves in a spectacular shade of crimson. Papers tied to the lower branches twisted in the breeze.

Pam shook her head and smiled. The belief was apparently alive and well among the townspeople that the Wishing Tree, as they called this linden tree, held magical powers to grant wishes tied to its branches. She swallowed the growing lump in her throat. There was something very timeless and comforting about her hometown.

Pam turned away from the square and headed toward her grandmother's former home. She slowed as she passed by, noting the overgrown landscaping, sagging railing on the front porch, rusted gutters, and patches on the roof devoid of shingles.

Acid rose in the back of her throat. Was it still owned by the young family that had bought the house after her grandmother had died? If so, why weren't they maintaining the home?

Pam made a U-turn and drove back to the house, parking at the curb of the well-kept home next door. She felt like she did when she saw photos of a person whose body had been ravaged by a chronic disease— sad and powerless to alter the outcome.

She sat in her car, squinting at the façade, and conjured up memories of working with her grandmother in the now untended garden. The sugar maple in the backyard rose above the house, its vibrant orange-red leaves starkly contrasting the dingy grey siding.

A pickup truck bearing the logo "Right Way Realty" stopped in front of her grandmother's former residence.

A man got out of the truck and unloaded a large white L-shaped wooden bracket.

Pam gasped and flung her car door open. She raced up to the man without pausing to close her car door. "What're you doing?"

He set the bracket down in the middle of the dormant lawn, five feet in from the street. "I'm installing a for-sale sign."

"Why're you doing that?" Pam's voice sounded shrill to her own ears.

The man looked at her.

She raked her fingers through her hair. "Okay—I understand. Someone's putting it on the market."

"Not someone," he replied. "The bank. This house got foreclosed last week. The bank's hired Right Way to sell it."

"*No!*" Pam was astounded by her reaction.

"Was…this your house, miss? Did you get fore-closed?" His tone was gentle. "I know this must be…"

"No—it's not that." Pam filled her lungs with crisp air. "My grandmother owned this house when I was growing up. I've got such fond memories of it." She swiveled her head to look at it. "And I want to buy it."

Even though she hadn't considered the words surfacing from the deepest part of her, the moment she uttered them, she recognized how right they were. She would create a new life in the place that had always been home.

The man picked up the sign from the truck bed. "You can get our phone number from here." He pointed to the sign. "The house will be listed on the MLS tomorrow."

"I want to buy it now—today." She grabbed the other end of the sign.

They stood, each holding an edge of the sign and staring at the other.

"Miss," he said, "I have to finish hanging this sign."

"Can't you wait?" She pulled her phone out of her pocket with one hand while maintaining her death grip on the placard. "I'm going to call"—she looked at the sign as she punched in the phone number— "the listing agent right now." She flashed the man her brightest smile.

He pursed his lips.

"Hello," she said as the agent answered the call. "I'm interested in making a preemptive offer on a house you're planning to put on the market tomorrow." She listened and then began nodding her head vigorously. "I can afford that," she replied. "And I won't need to view the inside. I know every nook and cranny of this house."

Pam held the phone away from her face and addressed the man. "Give me ten more minutes, okay? We're working out a deal. When I'm done, I'll let you talk to the listing agent to verify that you won't be needing this." She raised her end of the sign.

The man's eyes widened, but he nodded his assent without another word.

Pam pulled into Irene's driveway at eight o'clock that night. The porch light was lit, and a colorful wreath of gourds and miniature pumpkins glowed in the warm orb of its illumination.

Pam took a deep breath and allowed herself to sink

against the seat. What in the world had she just done? A feeling of warmth and contentment radiated from her heart to her fingertips. She'd just bought the house that was a repository of wonderful memories for her and where she'd make a lifetime of new, happy memories.

Pam texted her mother that she had arrived. She got out of the car and headed up the walkway.

Irene threw the door open and ran down the steps, arms outstretched, to greet her daughter.

"I'm so glad you're here," Irene said as she kissed Pam's cheek. "Thank you for letting me know you were going to be late. I would have been worried sick."

"Of course," Pam said. "Did you eat?"

Irene nodded. "I made a big batch of soup. Can I warm you up a bowl?"

"I'd love that," Pam said.

"And you'll tell me what you've been up to? Your message was so cryptic."

"I certainly will. I think you're going to love what I've done."

"I'm glad you're back home," Irene said, hooking her arm around Pam's waist and drawing her up the steps. "Even if it's only for a little while."

Pam grinned at her mother. "Funny you should say that. Wait until you hear..."

➤))⟫

Thank you for reading an introduction to *WORKOUT WISHES & VALENTINE KISSES*, Book 4 of The

Wishing Tree series, available here. Keep reading for a glimpse into each of the books in the series. You won't want to miss a book in this wonderful new collection from a group of best-selling authors, who are all founding authors of My Book Friends.

A PARADE OF WISHES

CAMILLE DI MAIO

A PARADE OF WISHES

The doorman tipped his black top hat as Liz Guidry approached the door. The lapels of his woolen coat were embroidered with red thread that mimicked the logo of the twelve-story Park Avenue building. A second doorman sat at a reception desk surrounded by small screens that revealed every corner of the building's public spaces in crisp black-and-white detail.

The address was duly prestigious, but it was really the presence of *more* than one attendant that laid the clue as to the exclusivity of the place. Liz had once had a commission at 25 Columbus Circle— the left tower housing apartments and the right boasting the five-star Mandarin Oriental Hotel. That address had *four* doormen all at the same time. One for the elevator, one for the reception desk, one to open the lobby door, and one to open the car door of the private sedan hired to take you about town.

This building was much smaller than the other, though, so two was more than sufficient.

It was a case of good cop/bad cop. The man at the door welcomed her with holiday cheer befitting of the ceiling-height tree in the lobby. The man at the desk smiled with his mouth but glared with his eyes as if her intentions were suspect. He must be new— she'd been here almost daily for the last four weeks.

"Elizabeth Guidry," she said, feeling a chill flush though her that was not due to the frigid weather outside.

He typed her name into a computer, and she must have passed the test because he waved her toward the ornate elevator at the end of the lobby.

A blast of cold air filled the space as another person entered. From the sound of the delicate footsteps, Liz assumed that it was a woman.

"Neva Cabot," she heard. The voice had a musical quality.

Liz smelled her before she saw her, which outside of New York might be a funny thing to consider, but since eye contact with strangers was a rare commodity, all the other senses came together to form an impression. In this case, it was a waft of vanilla and cinnamon, cozy and homemade, and nothing like the samples Liz had been given at various counters at Macy's and Nordstrom.

Liz entered the elevator first and caught a glimpse of her companion as the mirrored doors closed. Hair long and silvery. Arms adorned with what appeared to be friendship bracelets and wooden bangles. Feet warmed with knockoff Uggs, even though the brand had long ago lost some of its panache in this sort of neighborhood.

"White Christmas" as interpreted by saxophone drifted through the speakers.

"Heading to Patricia's?" the woman asked. The musical lilt to her voice was even more pronounced this close, and the overall impression she left was *ethereal.*

Liz could not remember meeting many people in New York who could be described as ethereal.

"Yes," she answered.

"I'm her godmother," she said with obvious pride. "One of them, at least. Her mother and I were childhood friends."

Liz had met Patricia's mother, Stella Markhouse, also of Park Avenue. Also of this building. The penthouse, in fact. The furthest thing from *ethereal* that Liz could imagine. *Dowager* was more like it. Fitting, too, as she was a widow three times over if Page Six was to be believed.

Liz would not have imagined that these two women would be friends, let alone call the same planet home.

"How nice," she responded noncommittally.

"I know what you're thinking," the woman laughed. "And you'd be right. Stella's origins were humble like mine, though she'd never admit it."

Liz's curiosity was piqued, but the woman spoke again before she could follow up.

"And how do you know our dear Patricia?"

"I'm the muralist."

"Ah!" Neva Cabot clapped her hands and the wooden bracelets clanked together like Dutch clogs. "Elizabeth Guidry. The artist whom everyone talks about. Stella sent me a copy of the writeup about you in *In Style*: 'Out with Nature vs. Nurture, the Nursery is the Thing!'"

"Yes," Liz said, her cheeks warming. She had painted the nursery for the cousin of the editor in chief last year and had been featured in a later issue. Ever since then, she received no less than twenty inquiries a day from young mothers who *simply had* to have Elizabeth paint a scene in their precious children's nursery. So far, she'd covered fairy tale themes, woodsy scenes, circus extravaganzas, and even pastel race cars. She interviewed clients, dug into what made them tick (it usually wasn't what they said but what they didn't say), and then, like a big reveal on HGTV, surprised them in the end with an over-the-top creation on their four walls that immersed the baby into the world that she'd created. She didn't stop at paints— if you looked closely, she incorporated tactile pieces that could grow with the child—leather, satin, twigs, mirrors— anything that delighted and was large enough to not be a choking hazard if Johnny or Suzie ripped it from the wall.

The elevator dinged. The eleven floors had passed by with the pace of a tortoise. It was the one thing in the building that had never been upgraded because it was an Otis original and therefore quite valuable as it was.

"I can't wait to see what you've come up with," Neva said as they stepped into the foyer-before-the-foyer. "Stella has been crazed with curiosity."

Then, she leaned in and whispered as they heard voices buzzing from behind the double doors. "Between you and me, you're a brave girl to have taken the commission on. Patricia is a doll, but Stella— and don't think I don't love her— is not so easy to please."

Liz could tell that the woman meant it as a compliment, but it deepened the many butterflies that had been upsetting her stomach all day. The big reveal was like opening night of a one-woman Broadway show. The entire thing rested on her shoulders. If they liked it, the success was hers. If they didn't— she owned the failure.

She'd not had a failure yet. But there had to be a first time.

The butler opened the door before they could knock, and Liz was certain that the doorman at the desk had called to announce their arrival.

"Miss Guidry," he said formally.

"Marvin," she responded. And then she slipped him a paper bag. Scones from Tea and Sympathy. Clotted cream and strawberry jam in plastic to-go containers. The burly British man had confided his homesickness to her on one of her workdays, and she'd been bringing him treats from the six-tabled restaurant every time she was down in Greenwich Village.

Unlike the doorman at the desk, his mouth remained still but his eyes twinkled. Stella Markhouse believed that all *the help* should be void of personality, something she insisted for Patricia's home as well since Markhouse money paid for them.

"Elizabeth Guidry!" Mrs. Markhouse said from across the room, exaggeratedly loud enough for everyone to hear, as if to highlight that among the many requests that Liz received, *she* had been among the chosen.

Well, Patricia had. Liz had liked her from the first moment of the interview. But there was no doubt that this was Stella Markhouse's baby. Even if the *real* baby — the one that Patricia was due to pop out any day— was the rightful star of the show.

Stella kissed Neva on both cheeks but quickly left her behind to lead Liz around the room by hand and introduce her to the fifty or so people she'd invited to witness the occasion.

Patricia sat in the corner, her rounded belly resting on her lap. She looked uncomfortable physically and seemed miserable in spirit as the Who's Who swirled around her living room only thinly disguising their real aim of networking while almost completely ignoring the mother-to-be. She drummed her fingers on a book that sat on the table next to her, and although Liz couldn't see the title, she could easily tell that Patricia would prefer to be sitting alone and reading.

A waiter brought Liz a glass of pink champagne,

and she gulped it down in one swallow, without a care about how *gauche* it was. She needed to calm her nerves because, at their initial meeting, Stella had embarked on a soliloquy of dazzling ideas for the nursery. Ballerinas at the Met! Monet watercolors come to life! Paris scenes! All good ideas. Very Stella.

But not, as Liz observed, very Patricia.

After an excruciating hour, Stella clapped her hands and commanded the attention of her guests.

"Darlings," she projected. "This is the moment we've all been waiting for. Thank you for joining us for this momentous occasion. And thank you to the media outlets who responded to my press release. I am as excited as you are to see what the amazing Elizabeth Guidry has dreamed up for my little grandchild."

Patricia was standing next to her, and Stella patted her stomach.

"Now, we can't all go in at once, but don't worry, we've set up a camera that will play on the television screen so those of you in here can enjoy the moment with the rest of us. Come, come."

She led the way, Patricia and Liz following, and Liz was pleased to see that Neva had seemed to make the cut of the first round of people.

They entered the unfurnished room. The crib and dresser and rocking chair— all selected in neutral tones so as to not upstage the mural— had been moved to storage for the day. A makeshift curtain hung on the walls, and Liz had insisted that Patricia was the one to pull the rope off.

The room stilled and Liz dug her hands in her pockets as she waited for the reactions.

Stella was appalled. Just as Liz knew she would be.

But Patricia... Patricia looked exactly as Liz had hoped. She spun around slowly in obvious wonder, and when her gaze at last rested on Liz, there were tears in her eyes.

Thank you, she mouthed, away from her mother.

Liz just nodded. This made the risk all worth it.

For she had not acquiesced to any of Stella Markhouse's whims but to her own observations of Patricia, always looking as if she'd prefer to be hidden behind the pages of a book.

Instead, she'd painted a library. A magical library where six-foot shelves were painted. The wood grain considered in careful detail with book spines lettered in gold leaf. And above those, five feet of pure whimsy as cows jumped over moons and bunnies read in rocking chairs and little engines puffed up steep hills and little bears ate out of honeypots. They were embellished with tule and copper and twinkling lights and other items of whimsey.

It was more detail than Liz had ever embarked upon, fueled, she knew, by her wanting so very much to make Patricia know that she'd been seen. That she'd been known.

She had never been more pleased with her work.

"My dear," the musical voice said from behind. Neva took her hand and leaned in. "You have done an extraordinary thing here. In fact, I am hoping that I can entice you with a commission of my own."

※

Thank you for reading an introduction to *A PARADE OF WISHES*, Book 5 of The Wishing Tree series, available here. Keep reading for a glimpse into each of the books in the series. You won't want to miss a book in this wonderful new collection from a group of best-selling authors, who are all founding authors of My Book Friends.

CAREFUL WHAT YOU WISH

ASHLEY FARLEY

CAREFUL WHAT YOU WISH

Mary suspects her husband is having an affair. The hint of floral perfume lingers on his clothes when he arrives home from work. He can't look her in the eye when seated across from her at supper. And when she tries to talk to him, his mind is a million miles away. But the most damning evidence presents itself one morning in early June.

Mary is transferring laundry from her hamper to the washing machine when she discovers a pair of black lace panties in the pocket of Orville's work pants. Mary doesn't own frivolous undergarments. Perhaps if she did, her marriage wouldn't be in trouble. With a start, she realizes this isn't true. Nothing could've saved their marriage. Except a child.

Mary traipses off to work with shoulders slumped and head lowered. At the corner, she turns and looks back down her tree-lined street at the stately houses and manicured lawns. She's lived in her family's ancestral home on Wisteria Lane most of her life. Except for the twelve months after her wedding. The year before her parents died in a car accident that left Mary the house.

Her two-story wood-framed house is one of the largest on the street. But also, the one in most need of repair. An outsider wouldn't notice the deterioration. But Mary is all too aware of the rotting shutters, peeling paint, and crumbling brick steps leading to the wide front porch. Orville and Mary can barely make ends meet, let alone fork out tens of thousands of dollars for the improvements.

Mary tilts her face to the sky. Despite the early-morning chill, the sun is warm, the promise of a pleasant summer day ahead. She continues north for two blocks to the town square. Mary has never owned a car. Never needed one. In addition to a variety of restaurants and cafes, all the essentials are located either on the square or down on Main Street. Town Square Books. Duncan's Hardware. Luther's Pharmacy. Twice a month she borrows Orville's pickup and makes a grocery run to the Walmart on the outskirts of town. In the interim, Mary buys her fresh produce and meats at the Corner Market.

Mary silently mocks the fools pinning wishes to the town's famous Wishing Tree. The tree is a fraud. A gimmick to attract tourists to the area. Every day for a decade, Mary pinned a wish to the tree. The same wish. A plea for a miracle baby.

Mary turns east toward the residential section of

Main Street where the town's oldest homes are located. Her employer, Daisy Crawford, and her family live in the biggest and prettiest house.

Daisy is drinking coffee and reading the newspaper at the kitchen table when Mary arrives. She glances up. "What's with the gloomy face, Mary May? Is something wrong?"

Mary forces a smile. "I'm fine. I didn't sleep well last night."

Daisy snaps, "Get some caffeine. I won't tolerate your sour mood."

"Yes, ma'am," she says. But instead of pouring a cup of coffee, she takes her lunch box and purse to the laundry room.

Daisy leads an active social life. But Thursdays are her designated administrative days. She works in her home office, paying bills, responding to emails, and planning parties. Mary isn't in the mood to fake nice. She'll need to stay out of Daisy's way today.

Mary takes her bucket of cleaning supplies upstairs and spends the morning changing bed linens and scrubbing bathrooms. She stews over her problem while she works. If only she had someone to talk to. Her only friends are the wives of Orville's friends. And they will certainly take his side. Perhaps they've already met the owner of the black panties.

At noon, she retreats to the laundry room, where she picks at her tuna sandwich while washing and folding clothes and bedsheets. Even her favorite soap opera, usually the highlight of her day, doesn't distract her from her dilemma. When the laundry is finished, she grabs the broom and goes outside to the porch for some fresh air.

She's so lost in her thoughts she doesn't hear Daisy emerge from the house. "Mary May! What on earth are you doing? I've been watching you through the window. You've been sweeping that same spot for the past ten minutes. You're gonna sweep the paint off the floor."

Tears fill Mary's eyes.

"Oh, honey. What's wrong?" Daisy says in a tone of genuine sincerity that surprises Mary and makes her cry harder.

"My husband is cheating on me," she manages through sobs.

Daisy's expression hardens. "Why, that rotten . . . Give me that." She snatches the broom away from Mary. Taking her by the hand, she drags Mary into the kitchen. "Sit down. I'll make you some iced tea."

Daisy goes to the refrigerator for the pitcher of tea. She fills two glasses with ice and tea and sits down in the chair beside Mary. "Are you absolutely certain he's having an affair?"

Staring down at her glass, Mary nods. "I found lacy underwear in his pocket when I was doing the laundry this morning."

"What are you going to do?"

Mary shakes her head. "I've been trying to figure that out. If I confront him, he'll deny it. I need evidence of his affair."

Daisy's face lights up. "Then get it. We'll go on a spy mission. I can try out my new zoom lens. Where is Orville now?"

"At work." Mary glances at her watch. "His shift ends in fifteen minutes."

Daisy jumps to her feet. "I'll grab my camera and meet you in the car."

Mary places their glasses in the dishwasher, retrieves her purse from the laundry room, and goes out to the garage. On the drive to the outskirts of town, Daisy talks excitedly about hiding in bushes and peeking through windows. This is a game for her. But this is Mary's life, the end of her marriage.

Orville is emerging from the building when they arrive at the auto parts store. Daisy follows his truck several blocks to an undesirable neighborhood. Her white Mercedes convertible sticks out like a sore thumb amongst the ramshackle houses and clunker automobiles. Orville pulls into the dirt driveway of the nicest house on the street, a tidy little dwelling with pale blue siding and a yellow front door.

Daisy pulls to the curb across the street, and they watch Orville get out of his truck and hurry up the sidewalk. The yellow door swings open, and a very young, very pregnant woman steps into his outstretched arms. Daisy focuses her lens and presses the shutter button, recording Orville as he strokes his lover's enormous belly.

Daisy places her camera in her lap and speeds off toward town. When they arrive back at Daisy's house, she says, "Take the rest of the day off. Tomorrow, too, if you need it." She ejects the memory card and hands it to Mary. "Take this to the photo counter at Luther's. They'll make prints for you. But bring me back the memory card. Those things are expensive."

Afraid to trust her voice, Mary mumbles a thank you and gets out of the car. She fights back tears as she makes her way to the square. The gray-haired woman at the photo counter at Luther's looks at Mary with pity as she prints off the photos. When she hands Mary the packet, she says, "You're better off without him, hon."

On the short walk home, Mary removes the photos from the packet. Fanning through them is like watching a movie of Orville rubbing his mistress's pregnant stomach. Mary wonders if the baby is a boy— the son Orville always dreamed of having. She's not sure what hurts more, his cheating on her or him having a baby with another woman. The child Mary could never give him.

When she reaches home, Mary goes upstairs to her bedroom and stuffs Orville's clothes into two suitcases. She carries the suitcases downstairs to the kitchen, dropping them beside the back door. Brewing a cup of her homemade peach tea, she sits down in the ratty armchair by the window to wait. Darkness has fallen over the room by the time headlights appear in the driveway outside the window. Orville doesn't see her when he passes by the window or as he enters the kitchen through the back door.

"Where have you been?" she asks, and he jumps back, his hand pressed against his chest.

"Geez, Mary. You scared me to death. Why are you sitting in the dark?"

She switches on the floor lamp beside her. "I've been waiting for you. You missed dinner again."

"I went out with some guys after work."

She glares at him. "I don't believe you."

He lets out a sigh and drops to the matching chair beside her. "We need to talk. This marriage isn't working for either of us. I see how unhappy you are."

"I'm unhappy because I can't have a child. I'm not unhappy with you," she says, and thinks, *At least I wasn't until today.*

"We both need a fresh start. There's no mortgage on the house. Let's sell it and split the proceeds."

Anger pulses through her, sending Mary to her feet. "Are you outta your mind? This house belongs to me. I inherited it from my parents. And I'm not selling it." She drops the packet of photographs in his lap.

He stares down at the packet. "What's this?"

"Open it and see." Mary folds her arms over her chest and watches for his reaction.

His face falls when he sees the pictures. "Oh."

"*Oh* is right. I want you out of this house tonight. Your bags are already packed." She gestures at the suitcases waiting beside the back door.

He gets up, grabs the suitcases, and leaves without so much as a glance back at her. Stepping out onto the screened porch, she watches him round the back corner of the house and disappear through the side gate. He's gone. Their marriage is over. She has nothing to show for their twenty-five years together. No family. No savings. No retirement plan.

She crosses the porch and descends the steps into the backyard. She takes a deep breath of honeysuckle-scented night air and looks up at the twinkling stars in the inky sky. A glimmer of hope sparks within her. She has no money and no education to speak of. But she has faith in herself.

A fresh start is exactly what she needs.

Thank you for reading an introduction to *CAREFUL WHAT YOU WISH*, Book 6 of The Wishing Tree series, available here. Keep reading for a glimpse into each of the books in the series. You won't want to miss a book in this wonderful new collection from a group of best-selling authors, who are all founding authors of My Book Friends.

FROM THE AUTHORS

We want to thank you for reading this prequel that leads into The Wishing Tree series. We hope that you have enjoyed it and are ready to download the full-length novellas. For some of us, this was the first author series collaboration that we've been a part of, and what we can tell you is this, it's tricky but a lot of fun! One of our biggest strengths in the world-building was sharing a document with names of all the town characters and establishments in each of our books. We also found that once that was established, it was fun to take off with our own characters and their stories and overlap cameos from each other's characters where possible. We had so much fun, some of us are planning even more books to be set in Linden Falls so stay tuned for more!

THE WISHING TREE SERIES

Get all the books in The Wishing Tree series!

※》》

Book 12: Wishes of Home by Barbara Hinske
Book 13: Wishful Witness by Tonya Kappes

THE WISHING TREE BLURBS

I Wish...

Amanda Prowse

Wishes in branches tied with string. Someone's hopes. Another's dreams.

When heartache disrupts her world, Verity's life in London's affluent Chelsea is blown apart.

Hiding from the press and the pain of rejection, she and her teenage daughter, Sophie, pack their bags and head to Linden Falls, a small town in Vermont. It is here in this quaint New England neighbourhood that her journey of self-discovery takes an unexpected twist.

Verity begins to feel at home in the close-knit community and pretty soon realises that what she thought was an ending is about to lead to a whole new beginning. The question she asks the Wishing Tree is whether she will ever find the courage to listen to her heart and not her head...

Join Amanda Prowse, the best-selling World Book Night author as she brings the latest book in The Wishing Tree series alive, featuring Verity, who might find a new opportunity in Linden Falls.

※》》

Wish You Were Here
Kay Bratt

Wishes in branches tied with string. Someone's hopes. Another's dreams.

Henry Harmon has been married more than sixty years to his bigger-than-life and talk-of-the-town wife, Greta, when he begins to see signs of a problem. When her diagnosis comes to light, he struggles to keep his oath of in sickness and health and to do it alone.

On the other side of their small town is Neva Cabot, who many years ago put her own mental health first when she cut friendship ties with Greta. But Neva is the kindest of kind and has been the face of hospitality for their town for decades. Even so, it will take some soul-searching for her to be able to step up and help walk Henry through the hardest days of his life.

Janie Stallard and her two daughters have just moved into the old Johnson house when they can't make the next rent and will be forced to move out. Neva offers Janie a job and her family a safe haven while they figure out what they want to do, and Neva tries to figure out why they are really there.

Join Kay Bratt as she brings the latest book in

The Wishing Tree series alive, featuring Neva Cabot, the owner of the Wishing Tree Inn and the Curator of Wishes.

Wish Again
Tammy L. Grace

Wishes in branches tied with string. Someone's hopes. Another's dreams.

Paige Duncan returns to the small town of Linden Falls to seek the comfort of her hometown and her beloved mother. That contentment is short-lived when, after only a few months, she's faced with an unexpected and monumental loss.

In the midst of struggling to keep her mother's beloved bookstore afloat in the wake of her sudden death, Paige has the chance to grant a wish from the iconic Wishing Tree in the town square. She lost her trust in the tree long ago, but her mother's voice rings in her ears, reminding Paige that, when feeling disappointed, simply wish again.

Paige reluctantly agrees to bring her mom's therapy dog to visit the care center where her mom volunteered for years. As autumn creeps in, busloads of tourists and one special visitor arrive, and someone at the center reminds Paige that she is stronger than she realizes. Will her mother's advice allow Paige to believe in the magic of the Wishing Tree and second chances one more time?

Join Tammy L. Grace, USA Today Best-selling author, as

she brings the latest book in The Wishing Tree series alive, featuring a heartwarming story of love and loss and the hope of turning lost dreams into second chances.

Workout Wishes & Valentine Kisses
Barbara Hinske

Wishes in branches tied with string. Someone's hopes. Another's dreams.

Pam Olson and Steve Turner—childhood friends turned work colleagues—are perfect for each other. They just can't see it.

The personal trainers, who both work at the local gym, have a lot in common: a passion for fitness, messy divorces, and chemistry that neither will acknowledge. After a disastrous foray into online dating, Pam joins Steve in his no-dating pledge.

A happily married couple whom they train recognizes the attraction between the two and enlists the help of the Wishing Tree. The covert love mission comes to a head with a pledge-breaking blind date on Valentine's Day. Will tempers—or sparks—fly between Pam and Steve?

Join Barbara Hinske as she brings the latest book in The Wishing Tree series alive, featuring a heartwarming story of love, family, friendships, and the hope of new beginnings.

A Parade of Wishes
Camille Di Maio

Wishes in branches tied with string. Someone's hopes. Another's dreams.

Liz Guidry is New York City's It-Girl when it comes to painting murals in posh Park Avenue nurseries. But the accolades and wait lists are not fulfilling. Being around the families makes her want one of her own. When a mysterious woman commissions a different kind of piece, Liz drives it to Linden Falls, Vermont, where she encounters a local legend that leaves her skeptical.

Yet she can't deny the magic of the town's Wishing Tree when she draws a wish that leads her to a seaside village in nearby Maine, where a love she never expected to encounter awaits.

Join Camille Di Maio, Amazon Best-selling author, as she brings the latest book in The Wishing Tree series alive, featuring a heartwarming story of love, hope, and renewal.

Careful What You Wish
Ashley Farley

Wishes in branches tied with string. Someone's hopes. Another's dreams.

Mary May has lost her way. She's husbandless, childless, and soon to be homeless. She's lost her housekeeping job, and with no income, she can't afford the repairs on her family's dilapidated ancestral home.

On a whim, she ties a wish to the town's famous wishing tree. She doesn't expect her wish to come true. None of her many others have. And she's astounded when the maple tree in her backyard sprouts hundred-dollar bills.

After making the house repairs, Mary goes on a spending spree, purchasing a new wardrobe and fancy automobile. While the money buys the material goods she covets, it can't buy her the one thing she wants most. Friendship.

Mary's granted wish turns out to be both a blessing and a curse. Mary embarks on a journey to discover what message her Money Maple is sending her.

Join Ashley Farley, best-selling author of the Palmetto Island series, as she brings the latest book in The Wishing Tree series alive, featuring a heartwarming story of friendship and new beginnings.

Gone Fishing
Jessie Newton

Wishes in branches tied with string. Someone's hopes. Another's dreams.

Loretta Thompson is a people-person. She loves meeting new people and learning about their lives-- and she has a special gift which makes everyone she meets feel like she's their best friend. She periodically cleans rooms at the Wishing Tree Inn, and she's always been fascinated by what she can learn from the things guests leave behind. Her love of imagining the lives of lost objects leads her all over the country returning the misplaced items she finds at the inn. Along the way, she discovers a love of genealogy to match her whimsical imagination and the adoration of the camper she drives all over the country. After returning the last of her lost items, she picks up a couple of women she met years ago on one of her quests.

Sally Redwood was a genealogy center coordinator before she needed a hip replacement, and since she has no family where she lives, Loretta picks her up and takes her back to Linden Falls to help her heal.

And Lois Bryant has just lost her husband and needs a fresh start. She tells her children she's going to Vermont, and while they're not happy, Lois's spirits are refreshed and her mind is eased the moment Loretta pulls up with that silver camper in tow.

Back in Linden Falls, all three women tie a wish to the tree, each hoping and searching for different things. Loretta isn't sure why she's bothering with the string and paper, because the one wish that did come true turned out to be a disaster. When her amazing next-door neighbor of over twenty years moves and Loretta gets a new...grouchier neighbor, she marches down to the tree to remove her wish only to find it gone.

Of course.

Sally's wish is answered just as terribly, and when Lois's actually brings her estranged sister to town, Loretta vows she'll stop wishing altogether...

Join Jessie Newton, USA Today bestselling author of the Five Island Cove series, as she brings the latest book in The Wishing Tree series alive, featuring her typical heart-warming stories of enduring friendships, long-lost secrets, and created sisterhood.

⇛⟫

Wishful Thinking
Kay Bratt

Wishes in branches tied with string. Someone's hopes. Another's dreams.

Janie Stallard is carving out a new life for herself as the newest business owner in Linden Falls, overseeing a small shop called *Wishful Thinking*. In her spare time, she helps her aunt Neva run the Wishing Tree Inn. Things are moving along and as soon as Janie's divorce is finalized, she will finally be free to fully embrace all the changes. But is that what her heart truly desires?

Coco Baines is a guest in the Wishing Tree Inn and has only one priority for her stay; she plans to be in town (and in the gym) long enough to return to her job looking like the svelte anchorwoman her boss expects her to be, no matter how unfair she believes the outdated stereotype to be. She has to have that promotion!

When a rampant rumor in town becomes truth that a new business owner has bought the land the Wishing tree sits on and plans to take it down, the whole town is in an uproar. Even with Janie and Coco (with Neva

Cabot's help) both working hard to divert the crisis, it will take more than a few wishes to save it. A miracle is what they need.

Join Kay Bratt as she brings the latest book in The Wishing Tree series alive, featuring a heartwarming story of love, family, friendships, and the hope of new beginnings.

Overdue Wishes
Tammy L. Grace

Wishes in branches tied with string. Someone's hopes. Another's dreams.

Norma Braxton, a member of the Winey Widows and a retired high school librarian, is busy working on the All-Class Reunion in Linden Falls, when she comes face-to-face with a man from her past. A man who knows her secret. She's determined to pretend he's mistaken when he recognizes her, fearful that he could divulge what he knows and upend her quiet life. The life she's carefully constructed and led for the last fifty years.

He's persistent and doesn't leave town like she hopes, committed to learn more about the woman he remembers. Norma hasn't tied a wish on The Wishing Tree for years, but the appearance of the man she once knew, awakens something in her heart and leads her to the beloved tree in the center of town. Her wish is long overdue, but is there any chance of it coming true?

Join Tammy Grace, USA Today Bestselling

author, as she brings the latest book in The Wishing Tree series alive, featuring a heart-warming story of love, loss, and the hope of turning lost dreams into second chances.

※》》

A Whole Heap of Wishes
Amanda Prowse

Wishes in branches tied with string. Someone's hopes. Another's dreams.

Vera Brown is a well-known, much-loved character in Linden Falls. Her look is eccentric, ever-changing and comes courtesy of goodwill and thrift shop finds.

Her philosophy is simple, the prettier you make life, the prettier it seems. This serves her well when tending to the beauty needs and hair requirements of the ladies of Linden Falls. It also extends into her home life where her sunny personality, positive platitudes and warm welcome to all hides a deeper sadness.

Vera has a son, this much people know, and the rumour mill goes into overdrive as to why he is seemingly a dark shadow from her past, totally at odds with the sunny woman they know and love.

However, the folks from Linden Falls are in for a shock, because Vera announces that her son and his soon to be wife are coming home. And far from the image the gossips have conjured; her son, a college professor no less, is as charming as he is smart.

Vera, who is struggling with her low self-worth, is

anxious about inviting him and his fiancée back to her lowly trailer because in her heart she knows that she doesn't measure up, fearful that he left her behind long ago. This clever, cultured boy of hers. It's time for Vera to face her past, as she and her son try to build a bridge in time for his summer wedding.

Join Amanda Prowse as she brings another book in The Wishing Tree series alive in A Whole Heap of Wishes, featuring a heartwarming story of love, family, friendships, and the hope of new beginnings.

Wishes of Home
Barbara Hinske

Wishes in branches tied with string. Someone's hopes. Another's dreams.

On a dare, Pam Olson auditions to be the host of a local home improvement television show. She's already overtaxed with her busy physical training business, her budding relationship with her hunky fellow trainer, and remodeling her own old house. The last thing she needs is another commitment. But—sometimes—life puts your feet on a path you never expected.

Can Pam keep all the plates spinning, or will the thing she desires most crash to pieces?

Join Barbara Hinske as she brings the latest book in The Wishing Tree series alive, featuring a heartwarming story of love, family, friendships, and the hope of new beginnings.

Wishful Witness
Tonya Kappes

Wishes in branches tied with string. Someone's hopes. Another's dreams.

Join Tonya Kappes as she brings the latest book in The Wishing Tree series alive in Wishful Witness, featuring a cozy mystery that includes family, friendships, and a dash of humor in the hope of new beginnings.

ABOUT THE AUTHORS

AMANDA PROWSE is an international best-selling author whose twenty-six novels, non-fiction title and seven novellas have been published in dozens of languages around the world. Published by Lake Union, Amanda is the most prolific writer of best-selling contemporary fiction in the UK today; her titles also consistently score the highest online review approval ratings across several genres. Her books, including the chart-topping No.1 titles *What Have I Done?*, *Perfect Daughter*, *My Husband's Wife*, *The Girl in the Corner* and *The Things I Know*, have sold millions of copies across the globe. For more information, visit https://www.amandaprowse.com.

KAY BRATT learned to lean on writing while she navigated a tumultuous childhood and then a decade of domestic abuse in adulthood. After working her way through the hard years to come out a survivor and a pursuer of peace, she finally found the courage to use her experiences throughout her novels. Kay Bratt writes women's fiction, historical fiction, and small-town mysteries. Her books have fueled many exciting book club discussions and have made it into the hands of more than a million readers across the world. For more information, visit www.kaybratt.com.

TAMMY L. GRACE is the USA Today best-selling author of over twenty books, who brings readers unforgettable characters and perfect escapes in her binge-worthy women's fiction, whodunit mysteries, and sweet Christmas stories. She is a huge dog lover and includes them in all of her books, even writing two from the dog's perspective using her pen name of Casey Wilson. Her best-selling Hometown Harbor Series and Glass Beach Cottage Series are set in the picturesque Pacific Northwest, where readers can escape with a close-knit group of friends and their interwoven lives filled with both challenges and joys. For more information, visit www.tammylgrace.com.

BARBARA HINSKE is an attorney and novelist. She's authored the Emily series, *Guiding Emily* and *The Unexpected Path*; the mystery thriller collection "Who's There?"; and the beloved seven-novel Rosemont series. Her Christmas novellas include *Paws & Pastries*, *No Matter How Far*, and *The Christmas Club*, which was made into a Hallmark Channel movie of the same name starring Cameron Mathison and Elizabeth Mitchell (2019). Find her on social media and at https://barbarahinske.com/.

CAMILLE DI MAIO left an award-winning real estate career to become a full-time writer. Along with her husband of twenty-two years, she enjoys raising their four children. She has a bucket list that is never-ending and uses her adventures to inspire her writing. She's lived in Texas, Colorado, Pennsylvania, Virginia, and California, and spends enough time in Hawai'i and Maine to feel like a local. She's traveled to four continents (so far) and met Mother Teresa and Pope John Paul II. She just about fainted when she had a chance to meet her musical idol, Paul McCartney, too. Camille studied political science in college but found working on actual campaigns much more fun. She loves to spend Saturdays at farmers' markets and belts out Broadway tunes whenever the moment strikes. There's almost nothing she wouldn't try, so long as it doesn't involve heights, roller skates, or anything illegal. For more information, visit https://www.camilledimaio.com .

ASHLEY FARLEY is the best-selling author of the Sweeney Sisters series, as well as *Sweet Tea Tuesdays*, *Magnolia Nights*, *Beyond the Garden*, *Nell and Lady*, *Only One Life*, and other books about women for women. Her characters are mothers, daughters, sisters, and wives facing real-life situations, and her goal is to keep readers turning pages with stories that resonate long after the last word. In addition to writing, she is an amateur photographer, an exercise junkie, and a wife and mother. While she has lived in Richmond, Virginia, for more than two decades, part of her heart remains in the salty marshes of the South Carolina Lowcountry, where she grew up. Through the eyes of her characters, she captures the moss-draped trees, delectable cuisine, and kindhearted folk with lazy drawls that make the area so unique. For more information, visit https://ashleyfarley.com

JESSIE NEWTON is a saleswoman during the day and escapes into romance and women's fiction in the evening, usually with a cat and a cup of tea nearby. The Lighthouse is a feel-good, heartwarming women's fiction novel about best friends and the power of female relationships. Learn more at www.authorjessienewton.com

TONYA KAPPES has written more than 175 southern cozy mysteries, all of which have graced numerous bestseller lists, including USA Today and Woman's World Book Club pick twice . Best known for stories charged with southern charm, emotion and humor and filled with flawed characters, her novels have garnered reader praise and glowing critical reviews. She lives with her husband in northern Kentucky. Now that her four boys have flown out of the nest, Tonya writes full-time in her camper! You can find her all over social media and at Tonyakappes.com